Kingdom Principles

A Study of the Beatitudes

Chester M. Gross

Copyright © 2012 Chester M. Gross

All rights reserved.

ISBN:1500855774
ISBN-139781500855772

CONTENTS

	Acknowledgments	i
1	Poor in Spirit	1
2	Those who Mourn	12
3	Meekness	16
4	Hunger and Thirst	21
5	Merciful	26
6	Peacemakers	33
7	Persecuted	37
8	Insulted	43
9	Salt	47
10	Light	50
11	Kingdom Principles	53

CHAPTER 1
Poor in Spirit

What is commonly called "the sermon on the mount" is the first recorded sermon of Jesus in the Bible. It is not the first time he preached. We find Him in the temple reading from Isaiah before he began his ministry. Also when he was twelve he debated with the religious leaders.

The Beatitudes are the central expression of his teachings regarding the New Kingdom he has come to proclaim. It incorporates all the basic tenets of the New Covenant Christianity that was to be instituted when He shed His blood on the Cross at Cavalry.

The first Beatitude is the sum and substance of the whole sermon. Poverty of spirit stands in contrast to self-sufficiency and self-promotion. To be a Christian is to deny oneself and allow God to become one's everything.

We are taught by society that YOU should take care of YOU first. Jesus told us to love ourselves in the same manner and that we love our neighbors. Yet, scripture also teaches us to deny ourselves. The focus of what Jesus is telling us is not to be haughty or prideful.

Blessed in the original Greek means "happy", in the time of King James happy meant to have good luck or happen chance, therefore the early translators used the word "Blessed." But the actual translation is "happy are the poor in Spirit."

Being poor in spirit is to recognizing your need for God. The term poor is the same word used to describe the beggar Lazarus in reference to Abraham's bosom. This word means to be so destitute and poor that there is no way one could do anything to change his circumstances. It means to be completely destitute of one's own ability or self-sufficiency. This is the basis of the kingdom of God. No one can enter the kingdom of God without humility of heart.

To be poor in spirit also means to be humble, to have a correct estimate of oneself (Romans 12:3). It does not mean to be "poor spirited" and have no backbone at all! "Poor in spirit" is the opposite of the world's attitudes of self-praise and self-assertion. It is not a false sense of one self in abasement but being honest with oneself: to realize that without God we are utterly lost and without hope.

Matthew 5:3 "God blesses those who are poor and realize their need for him, for the Kingdom of Heaven is theirs."

The message bible says it this way. "You're blessed when you're at the end of your rope. With less of you there is more of God and his rule."

Every person has sinned and are in need of God' help. We all at one time thought of ourselves as the world thinks. "We can do this ourselves." Jesus wants us to realize that without God we are nothing and will never be able to overcome the obstacles we face in life. All mankind has fallen short of God's perfection and standard therefore we need Him, to be able to rise to a higher level. This can only be done by accepting that we are "poor in spirit."

Romans 3:23 "For everyone has sinned; we all fall short of God's glorious standard."

The only way that we can come into God's Kingdom is to come as a child. This reference is speaking about the attitude in which we are required to come. It must be without malice, or pride or self-ability. A child comes to his parent without any of these things and allows the parent to care for them. This is how God wants us to come to him. An infant is totally at the subjection and dependence of the parent. They cannot even feed themselves. This is total dependence on the parent for everything.

Matthew 18:3–5 "Then he said, "I tell you the truth, unless you turn from your sins and become like little children, you will never get into the Kingdom of Heaven. So anyone who becomes as humble as this little child is the greatest in the Kingdom of Heaven. "And anyone who welcomes a little child like this on my behalf is welcoming me."

Another trait we must have to come to God is humility of heart which requires us to give all of our worries and concerns to God. Understanding that we have an enemy which is watching and waiting for us fail and ready to pick us off when we walk in pride and self-sufficiency.

1 Peter 5:3–5 "Don't lord it over the people assigned to your care, but lead them by your own good example. And when the Great Shepherd appears, you will receive a crown of never-ending glory and honor. In the same way, you younger men must accept the authority of the elders. And all of you, serve each other in humility, for "God opposes the proud but favors the humble."

James 4:6–8 "But he gives us even more grace to stand against such evil desires. As the Scriptures say, "God opposes the proud but favors the humble." So humble yourselves before God. Resist the devil, and he will flee from you. Come close to God, and God will come close to you. Wash your hands, you sinners; purify your hearts, for your loyalty is divided between God and the world."

The "Kingdom of God" referred to in this reference is the "rule or reign of God in the heart and life of a person or the earth system. The term Kingdom of God and Kingdom of heaven are the same thing. Matthew uses Kingdom of heaven and Mark, Luke and John use Kingdom of God. The term refers to the rule of God on earth or in one's life.

John 3:3 "Jesus replied, "I tell you the truth, unless you are born again, you cannot see the Kingdom of God."

Paul also writes that there are requirements to entering God's Kingdom. I want to remind you that we are not talking about heaven here. When talking about the Kingdom of God we are talking about the principles that make the earth work. They are principles or laws God has set in motion to govern mankind and the world we live in.

1 Corinthians 6:9–10 "Don't you realize that those who do wrong will not inherit the Kingdom of God? Don't fool yourselves. Those who indulge in sexual sin, or who worship idols, or commit adultery, or are male prostitutes, or practice homosexuality, or are thieves, or greedy people, or drunkards, or are abusive, or cheat people—none of these will inherit the Kingdom of God."

When the Bible talks about not entering the Kingdom of heaven or the Kingdom of God He is not saying we will not go to heaven but rather that the Word of God or the principles of the Kingdom will not work for us if we live in this lifestyle.

Those who are dependent on God (poor in spirit) the principles of the Kingdom will work for them. Christians tend to make everything about obedience to rules and most of those rules come from the Old Covenant not the New Covenant, which becomes legalism. What Jesus is teaching us to do is to walk in the principles of the Kingdom of God which he came to institute. Old Testament legalism brought the wrath of God. The principles of the New Covenant Kingdom produce fruit if one applies them and nothing if not applied.

Matthew one of Jesus disciples declares that we must seek his Kingdom first and his righteousness, and then all these things will be given to you as well."

Romans 14:17 "For the Kingdom of God is not a matter of what we eat or drink, but of living a life of goodness and peace and joy in the Holy Spirit."

Jesus is reminding us that God's Kingdom is not found from what we eat or what we do. It can only be found when we operate in the principles of that Kingdom. God's Kingdom principles are what make everything here on earth work. We sometimes wonder why our prayers are not being answered. One of the reasons, and certainly not the only reason is that we violate the principles of God's rule and authority on the earth. These principles are what determine whether we receive what God has promised to us.

Here is a couple examples of a principle of God's Kingdom at work. When Jesus was alone with the twelve disciples and the others around him they asked him about the parables he had just given to the crowd of people. He told them, "The secret of the Kingdom of God has been given to you. But to those on the outside everything is said in parables."

Jesus just shared the principle of the sower who sows his seed on the different kinds of soil and depending on what kind of soil he planted the seed in determined whether or not he would reap a crop from the seed he planted. The principle of the Kingdom of God is whatever you sow you will also reap. First you cannot plant seed for corn and harvest tomatoes. It doesn't work that way in the natural and certainly won't work that way in our spiritual lives. We will always harvest a crop from the kind of seed we plant. If you are believing for healing in your body, reading scriptures about end times will not produce the fruit of healing. The bible says the Scriptures are seeds so if you want a specific result or fruit from the scriptures in your life you must study and search for those promises and then apply them to your life.

A second principle, Jesus explains in another parable. A land owner rents his land to some tenants to care for His property and produce fruit from the land. They refuse to produce fruit so the land owner takes it away and gives the land to someone who will produce more fruit. This seems harsh to us, God taking something away from someone and giving it to someone else. This clearly shows us how important our producing fruit is to God.

Matthew 21:43 "I tell you, the Kingdom of God will be taken away from you and given to a nation that will produce the proper fruit."

These are just two of the principles of the Kingdom of God. For us to operate in the principles of the Kingdom of God we are required to empty ourselves of self and become completely reliant on God. Then we will inherit the Kingdom of God and walk in the blessings of that Kingdom.

Jesus expects us to produce fruit this is a requirement not a suggestion. If we as Christians refuse to walk in the principles God has laid out for us then they will be taken away from us. Most people would read this and think "if the Kingdom is taken away from me then I will go to hell. No that is not what he is talking about. Remember the definition of the Kingdom of God." The Kingdom of God is the rule and authority of God on earth. The principles of the Kingdom of God are what make everything work. Things do not work in our lives because we are violating the principles that make God's Kingdom work. It is not referring to heaven or hell.

The first principle is that we must be poor in spirit, we must come to God in a humble attitude understanding that all that He gives us we could not earn by our own efforts. We must be poor in spirit.

Chapter 2
Those who Mourn

Matthew 5:4 "God blesses those who mourn, for they will be comforted."

Matthew 5:4 "You're blessed when you feel you've lost what is most dear to you. Only then can you be embraced by the One most dear to you." Message Bible

This beatitude shows how a person who is right with God should conduct his life. The second blessing is mourning our sinfulness.

The first beatitude tells us that to inherit the Kingdom of God we must be destitute of our own abilities and completely dependent upon God for everything.

- Poor in Spirit is our attitude about ourselves.
- Mourning is our attitude over our sin.

Once we become aware of our lack of sufficiency we must then mourn over our sinfulness. To become a Christian one must repent of their life of sin against God. This principle of God's Kngdom is for us to move forward. To do this we must first be dependent on God rather than our own abilities. We must express sorrow for the way we have lived. To mourn is to feel or express grief or sorrow. It is to show the customary signs of grief for a death. To feel or express grief or sorrow for sin.

James 4:6–10 "But he gives us even more grace to stand against such evil desires. As the Scriptures say, "God opposes the proud but favors the humble." So humble yourselves before God. Resist the devil, and he will flee from you. Come close to God, and God will come close to you. Wash your hands, you sinners; purify your hearts, for your loyalty is divided between God and the world. Let there be tears for what you have done. Let there be sorrow and deep grief. Let there be sadness instead of laughter, and gloom instead of joy. Humble yourselves before the Lord, and he will lift you up in honor.

Let's break this down.

- God opposes (resists or battles against) those who are proud.
- Grace to the humble (grace is loving kindness and favor).
- Submit to submit to God's control.
- Resist (stand against) the Devil (the false accuser).
- Come near to God and .he will come to you.
- Wash your hands you sinners.
- Purify your hearts you double minded.
- Grieve (endure hardships), Mourn (sorrow for sin) Wail (weep)

- Change laughter to mourning.
- Joy to gloom, humble yourself.
- Then God will lift you up.

Mourning is part of the process of salvation. Without sorrow for our sin we would never come to repentance and be saved. God always responds to us when we humble ourselves. The second part of this attitude is that once we mourn and feel sorrow for sin we will be comforted. This word "comforted" means to give a person strength and hope, to cheer up. John the revelator tells us of a time in the future when God will himself wipe away every tear from our eyes. He will also remove death and mourning, crying and pain. This is the promise of God's kingdom, when we feel sorrow for our sins God will comfort us and come to our aid and give us strength. There will come a day when sin will no longer be a part of our lives.

Psalm 23 is one of the most used Psalms of David in the Bible. David declares in verse 4 that "even though I walk through the valley of the shadow of death, I will fear no evil, for you are with me; your rod and your staff, they comfort me."

2 Thessalonians 2:16–17 "Now may our Lord Jesus Christ himself and God our Father, who loved us and by his grace gave us eternal comfort and a wonderful hope, comfort you and strengthen you in every good thing you do and say."

Life is filled with struggles and problems. Everyone

goes through them it's part of life. One of the principles of the Kingdom is that when we humble ourselves and mourn over our sin God will have compassion on us and comfort us in all our troubles.

2 Corinthians 1:3–4 "All praise to God, the Father of our Lord Jesus Christ. God is our merciful Father and the source of all comfort. [4] He comforts us in all our troubles so that we can comfort others. When they are troubled, we will be able to give them the same comfort God has given us".

Now that we have been comforted we are called upon to comfort others. When we recognize our need for God (poor in spirit) and express sorrow (mourn) for our sin God will open the Kingdom to us and we will be comforted.

This is all about the beginning stages of salvation. Comforting comes by knowing that God has opened the Kingdom of God to us giving us eternal life. This is the hope we have in Him.

CHAPTER 3
Blessed are Meek

Matthew 5:5 "God blesses those who are humble, for they will inherit the whole earth."

Meekness is a word we do not use much today. It is mildness displayed in one's attitude and a gentleness of spirit. Meekness toward God is that disposition of spirit in which we accept His dealings with us as good, and therefore without disputing or resisting. Gentleness or meekness is the opposite of self-assertiveness and self-interest. It stems from trust in God's goodness and control over the situation. A gentle person is not occupied with self at all.

The meek are those who quietly submit themselves to God and to his Word and whom follow his directions. They comply with his designs, and are gentle towards all men. Who can endure provocation without being inflamed or angered by it? A meek person would return a soft answer when provoked. Meekness therefore is an attitude of gentleness in the face of struggle or pain.

Some translations use the word "gentleness" to describe meekness. In this setting its primary definition is its willingness to submit to God's authority and walk in a gentle spirit.

Psalm 37:11 "The lowly will possess the land and will live in peace and prosperity."

So there is a benefit from being gentle of spirit and of tempering ones reactions to provocation or suffering.

- Poor in Spirit is our attitude about ourselves
- Mourning is our attitude over our sin
- Meekness is about submitting to God's will

Notice the progression! 1) Is to recognize our need for God 2) Is to mourn over our sin, 3) Is to obey God and submit to his will.

Moses was known to have been the meekest man in the entire earth. Yet we see Moses destroying the Egyptian army. Smashing the golden calf and making the people drink it. This certainly does not describe a weak man. So meekness here is found in his obedience to God.

Numbers 12:3 "Now Moses was very humble—more humble than any other person on earth."

Peter shares a principle of God's Kingdom telling us that women are to walk in meekness of spirit. It is this meek, gentle spirit that is precious to God. He declares it is not the outward appearance that God considers precious but the inner beauty which comes from a gentle spirit.

As believers we are to walk in the spirit of meekness and gentleness.

Ephesians 4:1–3 "Therefore I, a prisoner for serving the Lord, beg you to lead a life worthy of your calling, for you have been called by God. Always be humble and gentle. Be patient with each other, making allowance for each other's faults because of your love. Make every effort to keep yourselves united in the Spirit, binding yourselves together with peace."

Psalm 25:9 "He leads the humble in doing right, teaching them his way."

We are also to put on meekness or gentleness as a piece of clothing. Meekness is something we wear and put on each morning. This is done in our minds it is not literal but rather a way of thinking. To become gentle and humble we must think gentle and humble. This is something we develop through the renewing of our minds. We are changing the way we think about things.

Colossians 3:12–13 "Since God chose you to be the holy people he loves, you must clothe yourselves with tenderhearted mercy, kindness, humility, gentleness, and patience. Make allowance for each other's faults, and forgive anyone who offends you. Remember, the Lord forgave you, so you must forgive others".

When we clothe ourselves with gentleness it causes us to make allowances for other peoples bad behavior and encourages us that we should forgive people who hurt us since God has forgiven us for the hurt we have caused him.

The gentle hearted will inherit the earth. This is a reference to the coming age in which God will make a new heaven and earth after the return of Jesus Christ. To inherit means to take one's rightful possession of something. In this case it is the control over the earth which God the Father will give us.

2 Corinthians 5:17 "This means that anyone who belongs to Christ has become a new person. The old life is gone; a new life has begun!"

2 Peter 3:10–13 "But the day of the Lord will come as unexpectedly as a thief. Then the heavens will pass away with a terrible noise, and the very elements themselves will disappear in fire, and the earth and everything on it will be found to deserve judgment. Since everything around us is going to be destroyed like this, what holy and godly lives you should live, looking forward to the day of God and hurrying it along. On that day, he will set the heavens on fire, and the elements will melt away in the flames. But we are looking forward to the new heavens and new earth he has promised, a world filled with God's righteousness."

Revelation 21:1–5 "Then I saw a new heaven and a new earth, for the old heaven and the old earth had disappeared. And the sea was also gone. And I saw the holy city, the new Jerusalem, coming down from God out of heaven like a bride beautifully dressed for her husband. I heard a loud shout from the throne, saying,

"Look, God's home is now among his people! He will live with them, and they will be his people. God himself will be with them. He will wipe every tear from their eyes, and there will be no more death or sorrow or crying or pain. All these things are gone forever." And the one sitting on the throne said, "Look, I am making everything new!" And then he said to me, "Write this down, for what I tell you is trustworthy and true."

Jesus is taking us through the steps in becoming kingdom people. First we must get saved by recognizing our need for God, realizing that we cannot obtain salvation on our own. Second, we must mourn over our sin and God will comfort us. Next, we submit to God so we will inherit a place in the new kingdom and the new heaven and earth.

CHAPTER 4
Hunger and Thirst for Righteousness

Matthew 5:6 "God blesses those who hunger and thirst for justice, for they will be satisfied."

The next attitude is to hunger and thirst for that which is righteous. Righteousness can be translated as justice or to be in right standing with someone. Blessed or happy are those who hunger and thirst for righteousness for they shall be filled.

In Matthew 5:6. Jesus taught us to seek his kingdom and his righteousness first. It was important to Jesus that we would seek for his kingdom before anything else in our lives. Let's recap the last three and add this fourth attitude.

- Poor in Spirit is our attitude about ourselves.
- Mourning is our attitude over our sin.
- Meekness is about submitting to God's will.
- Thirsting for Righteousness is about our attitude towards the Lord.

Jesus in speaking this series of blessings is moving us in a progression from preparing ourselves to be saved to what kind of people we should be. To Hunger and Thirst is to painfully desire that which will satisfy the hunger or thirst we have to God and his ways. It is to eagerly long for right standing with God.

Righteousness is a relationship with God where we are acquitted of our sins and brought into a right relationship with Him. In this process God imparts his righteousness giving us a brand new nature. This is why Second Corinthians states that if we are in Christ then we become a new creation, a new person because the old has gone and the new has come.

The reason Jesus came and gave us this incredible gift of salvation was so we could become right with God. Jesus came to restore the relationship with man which Adam lost when he fell from grace and ate from the wrong tree. Jesus took our sins and was nailed to a tree in our place to atone for the sins we committed. This was done so our nature could be renewed enabling us to live a righteous life.

1 Peter 2:24 "He personally carried our sins in his body on the cross so that we can be dead to sin and live for what is right. By his wounds you are healed."

Righteousness is a free gift given to us through Jesus Christ. Human effort cannot obtain it, nor can our attempts at trying to be good. In all this we fall short. Righteousness is not the way we act, but rather who and what we are. We are the righteousness of God in Christ, not because of anything we have done or even stopped doing but through what Jesus Christ has done for us.

Romans 5:17–18 "For the sin of this one man, Adam, caused death to rule over many. But even greater is God's wonderful grace and his gift of righteousness, for all who receive it will live in triumph over sin and death through this one man, Jesus Christ. Yes, Adam's one sin brings condemnation for everyone, but Christ's one act of righteousness brings a right relationship with God and new life for everyone."

Righteousness is a piece of armor which protects us from the attacks of the enemy. Without an understanding of righteousness we will be open to those attacks. Many people, who do not understand this truth, will continue to go to the altar to be saved every time they sin. Hebrews says that immature Christians are unacquainted with teaching about righteousness.

Ephesians 6:13–14 "Therefore, put on every piece of God's armor so you will be able to resist the enemy in the time of evil. Then after the battle you will still be standing firm. Stand your ground, putting on the belt of truth and the body armor of God's righteousness."

Our thinking has a great effect on the way we act. We must wake up our minds to become aware of our righteousness by spending time in the Bible. We must stop thinking failure, defeat, and sin. It is time to wake up to who we are in Christ.

1 Corinthians 15:34 "Think carefully about what is right, and stop sinning. For to your shame I say that some of you don't know God at all."

The Bible becomes our source of strength and teaches us about our right standing with God. The Bible reproves us, corrects us and encourages us. To learn of what righteousness is and how it affects us we must spend time reading the Bible.

2 Timothy 3:16–17 "All Scripture is inspired by God and is useful to teach us what is true and to make us realize what is wrong in our lives. It corrects us when we are wrong and teaches us to do what is right. God uses it to prepare and equip his people to do every good work".

People who hunger and thirst for righteousness will be filled up. This phrase "filled up," means to be full or to be satisfied in your desires. We are talking about the principles of God's Kingdom. When we walk in right living and stay in right relationship with God our desires will be satisfied. This is an incredible promise.

Psalm 37:4 "Take delight in the LORD, and he will give you your heart's desires."

Ephesians 3:18–19 "And may you have the power to understand, as all God's people should, how wide, how long, how high, and how deep his love is. May you experience the love of Christ, though it is too great to understand fully. Then you will be made complete with all the fullness of life and power that comes from God."

Philippians 1:9–11 "I pray that your love will overflow more and more, and that you will keep on growing in knowledge and understanding. For I want you to understand what really matters, so that you may live pure and blameless lives until the day of Christ's return. May you always be filled with the fruit of your salvation—the righteous character produced in your life by Jesus Christ—for this will bring much glory and praise to God."

Righteousness is one of the most important truths we can ever learn. It teaches us who we are in Christ. It helps us to understand what God expects from us and it changes our behavior. A righteous person lives a righteous life. It really is as simple as that.

CHAPTER 5
Blessed are the Merciful

Matthew 5:7 "God blesses those who are merciful, for they will be shown mercy."

- Poor in Spirit is our attitude about ourselves.
- Mourning is our attitude over our sin.
- Meekness is about submitting to God's will.
- Thirsting for Righteousness is about our attitude towards the Lord.
- Mercy is about our attitude towards others.

Jesus turns more directly to the character of his followers in relation to men; and in the next three Beatitudes mentions particulars which might be suggested by the sixth, seventh, and ninth commandments.

The mercy referred to here is not so much the negative quality which the word usually suggests, not dealing harshly, not inflicting punishment when due, sparing an animal or our fellow man. Rather it is an active kindness to the destitute and to any who are in trouble. It seems to lay more stress on the feeling of pity revealing itself in actions rather than just in our thoughts.

"Merciful" embraces the characteristics of being generous, forgiving others, having compassion for all who suffer, providing healing of every kind to all people.

This is what God has required of us, it is a principle of his Kingdom. When we practice these principles and make them active in our daily lives they produce the results which he desires. In this principle the merciful obtain mercy back.

Micah 6:8 "No, O people, the LORD has told you what is good, and this is what he requires of you: to do what is right, to love mercy, and to walk humbly with your God."

Jesus shows mercy by healing the sick. Mercy is an action not a thought; it reveals it's self by praying for those who are suffering and taking action to help relieve their suffering. We are not the healers but we are commanded to pray for the sick and minster to them;.

Matthew 20:30–34 "Two blind men were sitting beside the road. When they heard that Jesus was coming that way, they began shouting, "Lord, Son of David, have mercy on us!" "Be quiet!" the crowd yelled at them. But they only shouted louder, "Lord, Son of David, have mercy on us!" When Jesus heard them, he stopped and called, "What do you want me to do for you?[3] "Lord," they said, "we want to see!" Jesus felt sorry for them and touched their eyes. Instantly they could see! Then they followed him."

Mercy triumphs over judgment every time; all the time. Judgment destroys people lives. Christians judge more than they give mercy, it is what they are known for. It is our judgment that turns the world away from Christianity not our faith.

James 2:8–13 "Yes indeed, it is good when you obey the royal law as found in the Scriptures: "Love your neighbor as yourself." But if you favor some people over others, you are committing a sin. You are guilty of breaking the law. For the person who keeps all of the laws except one is as guilty as a person who has broken all of God's laws. For the same God who said, "You must not commit adultery," also said, "You must not murder." So if you murder someone but do not commit adultery, you have still broken the law. So whatever you say or whatever you do, remember that you will be judged by the law that sets you free. There will be no mercy for those who have not shown mercy to others. But if you have been merciful, God will be merciful when he judges you."

Remember the Pharisees judged everything. They had no interest in healing people or relieving the suffering of others. They just wanted to be the moral police and condemn people for violating their view of God's commands.

Moses vs Christ

It is interesting that Jesus spent so much time warning us not to be like the Pharisees. Yet the church today preaches the commands of Moses more than the commands of Jesus. This is how we become Pharisees. I have heard more sermons from the Old Testament than the New Testament. The law given to Moses was only a training tool to make us aware of sin and lead us to Christ. Now that we have Christ we are to follow HIS teaching over the teachings of Moses.

Mercy desires to relieve the suffering of others. Pharisaical thinking just wants to judge the actions of people rather than bringing healing to an individual.

John 8:4–11 "Teacher," they said to Jesus, "this woman was caught in the act of adultery. The law of Moses says to stone her. What do you say?" They were trying to trap him into saying something they could use against him, but Jesus stooped down and wrote in the dust with his finger. They kept demanding an answer, so he stood up again and said, "All right, but let the one who has never sinned throw the first stone!" Then he stooped down again and wrote in the dust. ⁹ When the accusers heard this, they slipped away one by one, beginning with the oldest, until only Jesus was left in the middle of the crowd with the woman. Then Jesus stood up again and said to the woman, "Where are your accusers? Didn't even one of them condemn you?" "No, Lord," she said. And Jesus said, "Neither do I. Go and sin no more."

Notice the thinking of the Pharisee as opposed to that of Jesus. This is a perfect example of mercy.

Matthew 9:10–13 "Later, Matthew invited Jesus and his disciples to his home as dinner guests, along with many tax collectors and other disreputable sinners. But when the Pharisees saw this, they asked his disciples, "Why does your teacher eat with such scum?" When Jesus heard this, he said, "Healthy people don't need a doctor—sick people do." Then he added, "Now go and learn the meaning of this Scripture: 'I want you to show mercy, not offer sacrifices.' For I have come to call not those who think they are righteous, but those who know they are sinners."

Jesus relates a story about three people. A Priest, a Levite and a Samaritan all who passed by the wounded man. A Priest was someone who served in the church this would relate to the Pastor today. A Levite was a helper to the Priest. Today he would be the Associate Pastor. The very people expected to show mercy walked past not caring that a man was suffering. A Samarian was of mixed race Jewish and pagan. The Jews were not allowed to associate or even talk with a Samaritan. It is not surprising that Jesus used a Samaritan to show the lack of mercy from the Priest and his associate pastor. It is often people who are not Christians which show more mercy to people. They care more about their community and the suffering of people. This is concerning because it is the job; God gave to the church.

I've had a thought for years of how Evangelists could impact cities for Christ but have never seen anyone do it. My thought is: What if each Evangelist coming into a city to do a large crusade would take ten percent of the money he or she raises in the meetings from that city and goes down to City Hall and asks what the greatest need of the city is? Then gives the city the money to meet that need. Scripture teaches that to help the poor is to honor God. Why are we afraid to support the secular? Sometimes they do a better job at ministering to the poor than the church. They are better organized and better funded because they work together as community. The church refuses to work together lest one church gets more credit than the other. This simply should not be. Mercy and caring for those who suffer is the ministry of the church.

Luke 10:33–37 "Then a despised Samaritan came along, and when he saw the man, he felt compassion for him. Going over to him, the Samaritan soothed his wounds with olive oil and wine and bandaged them. Then he put the man on his own donkey and took him to an inn, where he took care of him. The next day he handed the innkeeper two silver coins, telling him, 'Take care of this man. If his bill runs higher than this, I'll pay you the next time I'm here.' "Now which of these three would you say was a neighbor to the man who was attacked by bandits?" Jesus asked. The man replied, "The one who showed him mercy." Then Jesus said, "Yes, now go and do the same."

Jude 21–23 "and await the mercy of our Lord Jesus Christ, who will bring you eternal life. In this way, you will keep yourselves safe in God's love. And you must show mercy to those whose faith is wavering. Rescue others by snatching them from the flames of judgment. Show mercy to still others, but do so with great caution, hating the sins that contaminate their lives."

The merciful shall obtain mercy.

Hebrews 4:16 "So let us come boldly to the throne of our gracious God. There we will receive his mercy, and we will find grace to help us when we need it most."

The word "boldness" or "confidence" means to come with confidence or "freedom of speech". God wants us to come and feel free to talk to him when we are struggling. When we approach God with confidence we are promised mercy. When we seek to relieve the suffering of others God will relieve our suffering. What we sow is what we reap.

Remember what Mercy means, it is an active kindness to the destitute and to any who are in trouble. It seems to lay more stress on the feeling of pity showing itself in action and not only existing in thought. "Merciful" embraces the characteristics of being generous, forgiving others, having compassion for the suffering, and providing healing of every kind. If we want this kind of treatment from God we must treat others this way.

CHAPTER 6
Blessed are those who make Peace

Matthew 5:9 "God blesses those who work for peace, for they will be called the children of God."

- Poor in Spirit is our attitude about ourselves.
- Mourning is our attitude over our sin.
- Meekness is about submitting to God's will.
- Thirsting for Righteousness is about our attitude towards the Lord.
- Mercy is about our attitude towards others.
- Pure in heart is about our relationship with God.
- Peacemakers are about our relationship with people.

Peacemakers are the founders and promoters of peace who not only keep the peace, but seek to bring men into harmony with each other. A peacemaker is someone who loves, desires and delights in peace.

One of the great promises of the Kingdom of God is that we are given a peace which the world cannot receive. Jesus said that he would give us this peace so we would not be troubled or afraid. Somewhere I think the church has lost this ability to find peace. People are so stressed out that they cannot obtain peace in any kind of storm of life. I have discovered two ways to obtain this peace in my life. One, is to get on my motorcycle and find some curvy back roads and just ride. Second, is to turn on my iPod put some earbuds in my ears and close my eyes and allow the music to release peace. These things might not work for you but they do for me. Find your peace and when you do go there as often as you can.

John 14:27 "I am leaving you with a gift peace of mind and heart. And the peace I give is a gift the world cannot give. So don't be troubled or afraid."

Romans 8:6 "So letting your sinful nature control your mind leads to death. But letting the Spirit control your mind leads to life and peace."

As Christians we are expected to be at peace with other people. This is a principle of the Kingdom of God. To be at peace with people denies you the right to hold grudges or sustained anger. It requires us to release people from the offenses they have caused in us. It releases forgiveness which keeps us in peace.

Romans 12:18 "Do all that you can to live in peace with everyone."

Romans 14:17–19 For the Kingdom of God is not a matter of what we eat or drink, but of living a life of goodness and peace and joy in the Holy Spirit. If you serve Christ with this attitude, you will please God, and others will approve of you, too. So then, let us aim for harmony in the church and try to build each other up.

Galatians 5:22–23 "But the Holy Spirit produces this kind of fruit in our lives: love, joy, peace, patience, kindness, goodness, faithfulness, gentleness, and self-control. There is no law against these things!

Ephesians 4:3–5 "Make every effort to keep yourselves united in the Spirit, binding yourselves together with peace. For there is one body and one Spirit, just as you have been called to one glorious hope for the future. There is one Lord, one faith, one baptism."

Hebrews 12:14 "Work at living in peace with everyone, and work at living a holy life, for those who are not holy will not see the Lord."

The peace we are talking about can only come from God it does not come from people, or from the gathering of things. It is a kingdom principle and only can be released into your life through the power of God. James tells us that this peace which God gives is first pure (free from all faults), then it is peace-loving (it longs for and loves peace in all circumstances). It is considerate (treating others with respect), it is submissive (devoid of pride) and full of mercy (it releases forgiveness easily). It produces good fruit (good behaviors), it is impartial (it is fair and doesn't favor one person over another) and lastly it is sincere (undisguised or without hypocrisy).

James 3:17–18 "But the wisdom from above is first of all pure. It is also peace loving, gentle at all times, and willing to yield to others. It is full of mercy and good deeds. It shows no favoritism and is always sincere. And those who are peacemakers will plant seeds of peace and reap a harvest of righteousness."

In today's world how do we live without stress? Yet it must be possible if the Bible tells us not to be anxious about anything. It also gives us the secret; which is Prayer. When we pray we are leaving the problem in God's hands and releasing it from our hands. The kingdom principle here is that when we let it go and give it to God a peace which defies understanding will flood our hearts and minds and will also protect them.

Philippians 4:6–7 "Don't worry about anything; instead, pray about everything. Tell God what you need, and thank him for all he has done. Then you will experience God's peace, which exceeds anything we can understand. His peace will guard your hearts and minds as you live in Christ Jesus."

Those who sow peace shall be called the Sons of God. These qualities reveal to people that we are God's kids. Those who walk in peace experience and enter into the full privileges of their relationship with God. The term "Sons of God," is not gender related it is actually the children of God.

Having peace with God gives us the ability to come to God with confidence. Being filled with peace gives us the ability to be calm in the middle of a storm. Giving peace to others keeps us from bitterness and unforgiving. In becoming peacemakers we help other people find peace with God and with others.

CHAPTER 7
Blessed when Persecuted

Matthew 5:10 "God blesses those who are persecuted for doing right, for the Kingdom of Heaven is theirs."

- Poor in Spirit is our attitude about ourselves.
- Mourning is our attitude over our sin.
- Meekness is about submitting to God's will.
- Thirsting for Righteousness is about our attitude towards the Lord.
- Mercy is about our attitude towards others.
- Pure in heart is about our relationship with God.
- Peacemakers are about our relationship with people.

Being persecuted is about being Kingdom people, they are those who are harassed, hunted, spoiled. This term is used of wild beasts pursued by hunters. It is the condition of loss which people have been reduced to by persecution. They have "suffered the loss," possibly, "of all things," but they are "blessed.

People who are being persecuted because they live for God would also be heirs to the Kingdom. This relates back to Matthew 5:3 regarding the Kingdom and to

Matthew 5:6 regarding righteousness. The idea of this verse carries a bit of irony. These people were being persecuted because they were hungry and thirsty for righteousness. Their persecutors would be the religious leaders of Israel, the ones who claimed to strictly follow the way of righteousness. This seems to be the same today. Most of our persecution comes from within the church not from unbelievers.

Jesus tells us a story about a man who plants seed in four different kinds of soil. Only one out of the four produce any fruit from the seeds that were sown. This story represents a Kingdom principle. The principle is that if you sow your life into the wrong place you will not only have no fruit for your labor but you will also quickly fall away from the persecution of what you are trying to do. Persecution comes with the intent to attack us for doing right. Here in this story the man sowing seed may be trying to do right but he certainly doesn't understand Kingdom principles or he would not waste his time sowing in the wrong places. We do the same thing.

Matthew 13:20–21 "The seed on the rocky soil represents those who hear the message and immediately receive it with joy. 21 But since they don't have deep roots, they don't last long. They fall away as soon as they have problems or are persecuted for believing God's word."

Those who walk in the principles of the Kingdom of God also walk in the love of God. They understand the and know that there is nothing in all of creation including persecution that can make God love them less. This helps a Christian to be secure in their relationship with God. It also takes away the fear of punishment. Persecution cannot separate us from God's love.

Romans 8:35 "Can anything ever separate us from Christ's love? Does it mean he no longer loves us if we have trouble or calamity, or are persecuted, or hungry, or destitute, or in danger, or threatened with death?"

We are told to bless those who persecute us. This is something that must learned. Our human nature wants to curse those or attack them back. Instead, we are to speak a blessing over them. The importance of this principle is that God wants to keep our hearts and minds clean and clear of bitterness and un-forgiveness which will hinder us from receiving the promises of God and are known to cause sickness and stress. It is to our benefit that we bless people who persecute us rather than to curse them.

Romans 12:14 "Bless those who persecute you. Don't curse them; pray that God will bless them."

Next we are told to endure persecution. To endure is to refuse to react or retaliate against the person who is persecuting us. It has also been translated as being patient with those who persecute you. This Kingdom principle is aimed at our understanding that we are not of this world we belong to another kingdom.

1 Corinthians 4:12–13 " We work wearily with our own hands to earn our living. We bless those who curse us.

We are patient with those who abuse us. ⁱ³ We appeal gently when evil things are said about us. Yet we are treated like the world's garbage, like everybody's trash right up to the present moment."

The Apostle Paul had a problem which must have bothered him a lot because he asked God to take it away three times. There has been much speculation on what this problem might have been. I have heard everything from sickness to eyesight problems. Scripture doesn't mention sickness but does say a messenger of Satan was sent to harass him. One Bible translation calls this problem a thorn in his flesh. Paul realizes that even with this problem; God can still work in him giving him strength when he is weak so he delights in the persecutions, weaknesses, insults and hardships. The Kingdom principle is that no matter how hard life may become, life in God is still better. Our attitude determines our outcome. The Apostle James tells us to be happy when we go through many trials. Our attitude to persecution and hardships keep us free from bitterness and un-forgiveness.

2 Corinthians 12:10 "That's why I take pleasure in my weaknesses, and in the insults, hardships, persecutions, and troubles that I suffer for Christ. For when I am weak, then I am strong."

Everyone who wants to be godly will be persecuted. Someone always will disagree with our lifestyle. Most likely it will be fellow Christians but not always. They see our discipline as foolish and think we will judge them for their liberty. It is something we need to get used to when it happens. Stand your ground. It's not over until the trumpet sounds.

2 Timothy 3:12 "Yes, and everyone who wants to live a godly life in Christ Jesus will suffer persecution."

Jesus said he would become the cause for the persecution of the righteous ("because you are my followers," 5:11). The people who desired to be among the "blessed" of the Kingdom would not find their time on earth easy.

Why is it that we Christians believe that once we accept Jesus we should be exempt from suffering and struggle? Jesus told us to expect tribulation. He said we would be persecuted for his name. Peter said don't think it odd as though some strange thing has happened to you when you suffer. He also said that we were called to suffer just like Jesus did.

1 Peter 2:19–24 "For God is pleased with you when you do what you know is right and patiently endure unfair treatment. Of course, you get no credit for being patient if you are beaten for doing wrong. But if you suffer for doing good and endure it patiently, God is pleased with you. For God called you to do good, even if it means suffering, just as Christ suffered for you. He is your example, and you must follow in his steps. He never sinned, nor ever deceived anyone. He did not retaliate when he was insulted, nor threaten revenge when he suffered. He left his case in the hands of God, who always judges fairly. He personally carried our sins in his body on the cross so that we can be dead to sin and live for what is right. By his wounds you are healed."

The promise is that those who are persecuted will receive the Kingdom of Heaven. Again we are talking about the rule of God on earth and in our heart and life. Those who endure persecution without retaliating will walk in the principles of the Kingdom of God and receive the blessings of the Kingdom of God.

CHAPTER 8
Blessed when people Insult you

Matthew 5:11–12 "God blesses you when people mock you and persecute you and lie about you and say all sorts of evil things against you because you are my followers. Be happy about it! Be very glad! For a great reward awaits you in heaven. And remember, the ancient prophets were persecuted in the same way."

- Poor in Spirit is our attitude about ourselves.
- Mourning is our attitude over our sin.
- Meekness is about submitting to God's will.
- Thirsting for Righteousness is about our attitude towards the Lord.
- Mercy is about our attitude towards others.
- Pure in heart is about our relationship with God.
- Peacemakers are about our relationship with people.
- Being persecuted is about being kingdom people
- Insults build your character.

Verse ten speaks of the blessing for those who have suffered persecution and endured it, This verse speaks of the blessing of those who are suffering right now at this moment..

The word "insult" is used in the modern translations. The King James uses the word "revile." This word means to find fault with a person and blame them or discredit them. It also includes showing disproval and treating them as an object of contempt. The Kingdom principle is when people insult us and we do not retaliate we are building up our reward which will be given to us in heaven.

Luke 6:22 "What blessings await you when people hate you and exclude you and mock you and curse you as evil because you follow the Son of Man. "

Learning to leave things in the hands of God is the Kingdom principle. When insulted, threatened or suffering at the hands of other people we are to leave it in the hands of God.

1 Peter 2:23 "He did not retaliate when he was insulted, nor threaten revenge when he suffered. He left his case in the hands of God, who always judges fairly."

Respond to insults by giving blessing, by speaking positive things over them. The Kingdom principle is when we give blessing we inherit a blessing.

1 Peter 3:9 "Don't repay evil for evil. Don't retaliate with insults when people insult you. Instead, pay them back with a blessing. That is what God has called you to do, and he will bless you for it."

We are happy when we are insulted because of our relationship with God, not because of what we do or what other people do to us. So let's be careful that the insults and persecution are not because we are doing something which causes them.

1 Peter 4:14 "So be happy when you are insulted for being a Christian, for then the glorious Spirit of God rests upon you."

We are to be happy when people mock us, insult us and say bad things about us. Is Jesus really serious? Yes He is! So much so he says be happy and very glad because you have a reward waiting for you, and by the way you aren't the only people who were persecuted. They persecuted the prophets in the same way.

Matthew 5:11–12 "God blesses you when people mock you and persecute you and lie about you and say all sorts of evil things against you because you are my followers. Be happy about it! Be very glad! For a great reward awaits you in heaven. And remember, the ancient prophets were persecuted in the same way."

James 1:1–4 "This letter is from James, a slave of God and of the Lord Jesus Christ. I am writing to the "twelve tribes" Jewish believers scattered abroad. Greetings! Dear brothers and sisters, when troubles come your way, consider it an opportunity for great joy. For you know that when your faith is tested, your endurance has a chance to grow. So let it grow, for when your endurance is fully developed, you will be perfect and complete, needing nothing.

What an incredible future we will have when we learn to

put these Kingdom principles in operation in our lives. There is awaiting us an incredible reward when we get to heaven. What is the reward? We will have to wait to find out but we know it will be incredible.

CHAPTER 9
Being the Salt of the Earth

Matthew 5:13–16 "You are the salt of the earth. But what good is salt if it has lost its flavor? Can you make it salty again? It will be thrown out and trampled underfoot as worthless. "You are the light of the world— like a city on a hilltop that cannot be hidden. No one lights a lamp and then puts it under a basket. Instead, a lamp is placed on a stand, where it gives light to everyone in the house. In the same way, let your good deeds shine out for all to see, so that everyone will praise your heavenly Father."

To demonstrate the impact these people would make on their world, Jesus used two common illustrations: salt and light. Jesus' followers would be like salt in that they would create a thirst for greater understanding of God with other people.

When one sees someone who lives the principles of God's Kingdom and has these qualities in their lives they become salt and light to them showing them the qualities of God.

Salt refers to people who serve as a preservative against the evils of society. The important quality to note is that salt should maintain its flavor. If it fails to be salty, it has lost its purpose for existence and should be discarded.

Salt, by its very nature, flavors and preserves everything that it comes in contact with. If it did not do these things, then it would not be salt. Salt, a valuable commodity in the Middle East, it was used in the biblical period for barter. In fact the word "salary" comes from the Latin salarius ("salt").

When salt loses its flavor it becomes tasteless. The Greek defines salt losing is flavor as someone who becomes and acts like a fool

Salt is our witness that we are followers of Jesus because of the way we live and act. When people see the flavor of God in our lives they will see God himself.

When people see the salt of love they will know that we are followers of Jesus. When we love people it reveals a loving God. When we love each other, people can see the love of God.

John 13:34–35 "So now I am giving you a new commandment: Love each other. Just as I have loved you, you should love each other. Your love for one another will prove to the world that you are my disciples."

Helping one another is another way in which we can

reveal God to people. When the world sees our genuine care for each other they will be interested in the flavor of our lives.

1 Corinthians 12:24–26 "While the more honorable parts do not require this special care. So God has put the body together such that extra honor and care are given to those parts that have less dignity. This makes for harmony among the members, so that all the members care for each other. If one part suffers, all the parts suffer with it, and if one part is honored, all the parts are glad."

1 Thessalonians 5:11 "So encourage each other and build each other up, just as you are already doing."

When we act like unbelievers we are salt which has lost its flavor and this means we play the fool and become tasteless and will be tossed into the street to be walked on. We become useless to the Kingdom of God. When we love one another, encourage one another and help each other we show that we are following Jesus and people will be drawn to Christ.

CHAPTER 10
Being the Light of the World

Matthew 5:13–16 "You are the salt of the earth. But what good is salt if it has lost its flavor? Can you make it salty again? It will be thrown out and trampled underfoot as worthless. "You are the light of the world— like a city on a hilltop that cannot be hidden. No one lights a lamp and then puts it under a basket. Instead, a lamp is placed on a stand, where it gives light to everyone in the house. In the same way, let your good deeds shine out for all to see, so that everyone will praise your heavenly Father."

The Greek dictionary paints a picture of the light as a projecting stone in a wall of a house on which a lamp was set. The house consisted of a single room, so that the small light would give enough light for everyone to see. Even this one light allowed everyone in the room to see clearly. The contrast is that we so often think we must save the world. Here the verse is giving only enough light for those in the house. Those who are around us, in our inner circle. First that would be my family. What shall a man gain if he wins the whole world but loses his family? Our lives have enough light to light our house, and everyone who comes around us should be able to see clearly.

We are to keep the light of our lives open for everyone to see. Putting a basket over the light is pointless it puts the light out and makes the light useless. This kind of life does not glory God or share with anyone else the wonder of knowing Jesus

The point here is that our lives should glorify the Father. All these attitudes are behaviors which are to be seen in our lives. When people see these things in us it brings glory to God.

Romans 15:5–6 "May God, who gives this patience and encouragement, help you live in complete harmony with each other, as is fitting for followers of Christ Jesus. Then all of you can join together with one voice, giving praise and glory to God, the Father of our Lord Jesus Christ."

1 Peter 2:12 "Be careful to live properly among your unbelieving neighbors. Then even if they accuse you of doing wrong, they will see your honorable behavior, and they will give honor to God when he judges the world.

Finally to walk in the light is to do what is right. Those who do evil hate the light and refuse to go near it. This is why people refuse to accept God's invitation.

John 3:20–21 "All who do evil hate the light and refuse to go near it for fear their sins will be exposed. [21] But those who do what is right come to the light so others

can see that they are doing what God wants."

All of these principles bring blessing into our lives. They are behaviors which will produce fruit in our lives and will bring honor to God.

CHAPTER 11
Kingdom Principles

Kingdom Principles are rules which govern natural and spiritual law. I don't like using the word "law" because so many people take it back to the law of the Old Testament which brings punishment. Kingdom principles are meant to bring freedom not punishment.

The Laws of Moses were rules that carried grave penalties if violated and resulted in the punishment and wrath of God. Kingdom principles are the opposite. The restrictions they carry are meant to protect and bring freedom from the fear of God's anger.

Today I was Kayaking on a lake in Washington State. As I sat in the Kayak my wife and I were looking at the houses on the lake shore. One house had a deck on the upper floor. The deck had a railing around it to protect someone from falling off and hurting themselves. The purpose of the deck was to sit and look over the lake while eating with friends or just relaxing enjoying the wonder of God's creation. If the purpose of the deck was to be used as a diving board. Then the railing would be restrictive.

The purpose of Kingdom principles are not meant to judge or condemn when you do not obey them. If you violate them you will not go to hell, but there is a consequence if violated. It is much like planting seed in the ground and reaping the harvest. Whatever type of seed you plant will determine what type of fruit grows. Galatians also tells us that if we sow to the flesh we will reap death but if we sow to the spirit we will reap life. There is always a consequence to sin. Christians want to make laws which prohibit without understanding the purpose for which the law was given or how the law was intended to be used. The key to understanding the principles of the Kingdom of God is to understand why they were given and what they are intended to do. Galatians says "the law kills but the Spirit gives life."

When we think in terms of laws we misunderstand what Jesus was trying to teach us. The law of Christ brings freedom.

Romans 7:1–4 "Now, dear brothers and sisters—you who are familiar with the law don't you know that the law applies only while a person is living? For example, when a woman marries, the law binds her to her husband as long as he is alive. But if he dies, the laws of marriage no longer apply to her. So while her husband is alive, she would be committing adultery if she married another man. But if her husband dies, she is free from that law and does not commit adultery when she remarries. So, my dear brothers and sisters, this is the point: You died to the power of the law when you died with Christ. And now you are united with the one who was raised from the dead. As a result, we can produce a harvest of good deeds for God."

The principles of the Kingdom are built upon faith in Christ. Faith is expressed in a decision to accept Jesus Christ and his principles. Walking in the Spirit no longer walking in the natural.

Galatians 2:16–21 "Yet we know that a person is made right with God by faith in Jesus Christ, not by obeying the law. And we have believed in Christ Jesus, so that we might be made right with God because of our faith in Christ, not because we have obeyed the law. For no one will ever be made right with God by obeying the law." But suppose we seek to be made right with God through faith in Christ and then we are found guilty because we have abandoned the law. Would that mean Christ has led us into sin? Absolutely not! Rather, I am a sinner if I rebuild the old system of law I already tore down. For when I tried to keep the law, it condemned me. So I died to the law I stopped trying to meet all its requirements— so that I might live for God. My old self has been crucified with Christ. It is no longer I who live, but Christ lives in me. So I live in this earthly body by trusting in the Son of God, who loved me and gave himself for me. I do not treat the grace of God as meaningless. For if keeping the law could make us right with God, then there was no need for Christ to die."

Matthew 6:33 "Seek the Kingdom of God above all else, and live righteously, and he will give you everything you need."

If the kingdom of God was heaven then Jesus would not have told the disciples that they would be alive to see his Kingdom come. Jesus came and fulfilled the requirements of the Old Testament law and gave the world a new covenant based in his blood, introducing a new Kingdom with new principles.

Mark 9:1 "Jesus went on to say, "I tell you the truth, some standing here right now will not die before they see the Kingdom of God arrive in great power!"

Revelations 12:10-11 "Then I heard a loud voice shouting across the heavens, "It has come at last salvation and power and the Kingdom of our God, and the authority of his Christ. For the accuser of our brothers and sisters has been thrown down to earth the one who accuses them before our God day and night. And they have defeated him by the blood of the Lamb and by their testimony."

When we walk in the principles of the Kingdom of God all of heaven goes into action to fulfill the promises of God on our behalf. Walk in the Spirit and put on the attitudes of Christ and you are walking in the Kingdom of God.

Soon we will hear the voice shouting "It has come at last salvation and power and the Kingdom of God and the authority of his Christ. Soon!

ABOUT THE AUTHOR

Chester Gross pastors City View Church in Seattle, Washington. City View is a multi-ethnic and cross-cultural church. Members come from a variety of nations including the United States, Philippines, Africa, India and Mexico.

Chester's background includes living in the Philippines, overseeing over 600 churches as a missionary. He has been in ministry for 35 years, and pastored in the northwest, eastern Washington and Texas.

Chester teaches 3-4 conferences each year. To date he has taught Pastors from 28 different countries.

He is best known for his teaching on the Heart of the Father and Law and Grace. His teaching from a contextual model brings clarity and understanding to the Word of God.

Made in the USA
San Bernardino, CA
08 January 2019